United States Laws, Statues etc., Arthur von Briesen

Patents

A guide to inventors, manufacturers and merchants, who seek to secure

and maintain patents for inventions, trade marks and copyrights

United States Laws, Statues etc., Arthur von Briesen

Patents

A guide to inventors, manufacturers and merchants, who seek to secure and maintain patents for inventions, trade marks and copyrights

ISBN/EAN: 9783337286422

Printed in Europe, USA, Canada, Australia, Japan

Cover: Foto ©Andreas Hilbeck / pixelio.de

More available books at **www.hansebooks.com**

PATENTS.

A GUIDE

TO

Inventors, Manufacturers and Merchants,

WHO SEEK TO SECURE AND MAINTAIN

PATENTS FOR INVENTIONS,

TRADE MARKS AND COPYRIGHTS.

WITH AN APPENDIX CONTAINING THE
COMPLETE PATENT LAW OF THE
UNITED STATES.

BY

A. v. BRIESEN,

ATTORNEY IN PATENT CASES,

No. 258 BROADWAY,

NEW YORK.

EVENING POST STEAM PRESSES, 208 BROADWAY.

1878

-

INDEX.

INTRODUCTION.

No country in the world produces so many important and useful inventions and discoveries as the United States. This is to a great extent due to the liberality and wisdom of our government in securing to inventors by patents a protection for their inventions, thereby giving them an ample reward for the perseverance and labor, which they employ in making and perfecting the same. But, at the same time, the United States are careful that patents are only granted to those, who really deserve them. Only an *inventor* is entitled to a patent, one who has originated and produced *a new or improved machine or article of manufacture, or an improvement in the art of producing useful things, or a novel composition for useful purposes.* A mere imitator, and even he, who applies only mechanical skill to the amelioration of existing things, will not be entitled to a patent. In short, original mental work, in the direction of the industrial arts, is to be fostered and encouraged, but not the mere skillful use of known means and devices.

THE U. S. PATENT OFFICE

Is an institution of such magnitude, containing such a vast collection of monuments of the human intellect in the form of models, specimens, drawings, descriptions, etc., that it is altogether beyond the power of one mind to grasp the entire collection within its compass. Including foreign patents, our own patents, and rejected and pending applications, it contains a record of over one-fourth of a million of new inventions, relating to all the various branches of trade and industry. The building of the Patent Office is one of the most magnificent structures in the City of Washington. It is erected on two squares or blocks, and is situated on the principal thoroughfare. Nevertheless, it already proves too limited for the proper transaction of the vast amount of business carried on in it, and for the proper storage of the many thousands of models and records transmitted to it. It is at least to be hoped that the rooms now occupied in the Patent Office by the Secretary of the Interior and by the Land Offices will soon be surrendered to the Commissioner of Patents, and that a separate structure for the Department of the Interior will be erected.

THE COMMISSIONER OF PATENTS

is the head of the U. S. Patent Office. He superintends the examiners, clerks and other employés of the office ; decides controversies relating to the practice, and establishes rules and regulations, not inconsistent with the law, for the conduct of proceedings in the Patent Office. He is also the chief judicial officer, as all appeals arising in the office must be decided by him before they can reach the courts. In interference cases, the appeal to the Commissioner and his decision are final.

The applications for patents are submitted to the examiners, who are carefully selected for their learning and experience in the branches of the arts to which they are respectively assigned. They search into the merits of new applications, into the sufficiency of claims and specifications, granting and rejecting applications, as appears proper in their judgment.

To guard, however, against errors on their part, a system of appeals has been devised by law, whereby justice, to a meritorious inventor, is made almost a certainty. Three appeals are allowed ; the first to a Board of Examiners-in-chief, the second to the Commissioner of Patents in person, and the third to the Supreme Court of the District of Columbia.

The nature and cost of appeals are more fully explained under the head of " Appeals."

WHAT IS A PATENT ?

A patent is the guarantee of our Government that the originator of a new invention, or the person to whom he may transfer his right, shall, for the term of seventeen years, have the exclusive right to make, use, and sell the article invented by him. This guarantee is most liberally enforced by the United States Courts. In fact a patent is a contract between the inventor and the people, the inventor giving to the people a full knowledge of his invention, which the people, after the expiration of the patent, shall have the full right to use, and in consideration for the information thus imparted, the inventor receives for a limited time (17 years,) the exclusive right to use, make, and sell the improvement.

Patents are granted by our Government for every invention, which results in an actual new and useful improvement on an existing article, be it ever so small, or which produces new and original devices or machinery, compositions or processes, and it is frequently the case that apparently insignificant improvements yield large profits to the patentees, or to those who may have bought their patents.

Hundreds of patents are annually granted for such small improvements, and experience has shown that those inventions, which can be most readily introduced at a small expense, are apt to prove most remunerative.

That the patents for more important inventions are also profitable, and usually yield fortunes to the inventors or introducers, need hardly be mentioned. Everybody knows, that the owners of the sewing-machine, revolver, rubber, mowing-machine, electric telegraph, and other patents have acquired unlimited wealth. There is certainly no better opportunity for thoughtful and leisure minds than to invent. It is frequently the shortest road to fortune. But it is with inventors as with poets,—those least competent believe themselves usually the most expert, and mere imitators, copyists of other people's ideas, are generally the loudest to proclaim their titles as inventors. To sift the chaff from the wheat, to separate the true inventors from their parasites is the principal object of the Patent Office, its most laborious and often thankless duty, and the like duty of the courts, when they are called upon to decide controversies relating to patents.

HOW TO INVENT.

One who invents or seeks to improve existing devices should be particularly careful to *make himself well acquainted* with the state of the arts generally, and especially with that to which the contemplated improvement appertains, and with its defects.

Standard works on mechanics or other branches of science, in which the would-be inventor is interested, should be read and studied. This will enable him to go to work *knowingly*, where others trust to chance and good luck rather than undergo the labor which is necessary to lead to knowledge. If a new and useful invention has been conceived, a drawing, and, if the case admits of it, a small working model, should at once be prepared. This enables the experimenter to more carefully inspect and revise his invention and see whether it answers the purpose for which it is intended. He should not get impatient if some of these experiments prove failures. No really good and valuable invention has ever been made without the aid of study and perseverance. As soon as the invention is completed the application for a patent should be made without delay.

The model may be sent or brought to a respectable patent attorney, and his opinion as to the novelty and patentabilty of the invention obtained. At our office such opinions are frequently requested by inventors, who reside in the city, and also by those from the country, who send their models by express.

Every applicant may, when he selects an honest attorney, be sure that he will receive a candid opinion as to the merits of his invention.

Many inventors, from lack of energy, or from anxiety to select "more favorable opportunities," allow their inventions to "sleep," and fail to take early steps for securing their patents. This is a serious mistake, nay, it may be properly termed a fraud upon the public, which, holding out the broad protection of the patent, is entitled to an early and candid report of all inventions made. In the race of diligence between rival inventors—a race of more frequent occurrence than would be imagined—those are looked upon with most favor, by parties in authority, who display the most energy in bringing their inventions forward—not those who, like misers, hold them secure under lock and key.

Who can obtain a patent? Every person, whether a citizen of the United States or a foreigner, and all ladies and minors, who, having made an invention, whereby a new article is created for the trade, or an old article improved and its utility increased, may obtain a patent therefor, for the term of seventeen years. A patent is only granted to the person who can make oath that he or she is the *first and original* inventor, or, if there be joint inventors of the same thing, that they are the first original and *joint* inventors of the improvement for which a patent may be desired. Nearly all important articles of manufacture in the United States are protected by one or more patents. In many countries it has been deemed proper to grant patents to all applicants, without requiring the oath of invention, and to let the courts determine whether the patentees were really entitled to the patents issued to them. That under such a system the issue of many patents is but an idle performance, a mere farce, is self-evident; also that it is apt to invite piracy of inventions by unscrupulous persons, who do not shrink from appropriating to themselves the fruits of other people's labor. The wisdom of the American system, in requiring the solemn oath of invention, is therefore eminently wise and just, and has so proved itself by actual experience.

The Commissioner's Report for the year 1876

states that two-thirds of the manufacturing interests of our country are based upon _patents,
and that the welfare of all such interests is inti-
mately connected with the welfare of the patent
system.

During the past eight years a larger number
of applications for patents was filed and more
patents were granted than during the entire
seventy-eight preceding years, reaching back to
the enactment of the first patent law.   This
makes it evident that patents are profitable, for
otherwise the business of the patent office would
not have so wonderfully increased; and that
our system of granting patents is sound, else it
would not have become as popular, as the report
above referred to, shows it to be.

HOW TO APPLY FOR AND OBTAIN A PATENT.

Every person, desirous of obtaining a 'patent
for a new and original invention, should pre-
pare a model by which the invention is clearly
illustrated.   This model must not exceed one
foot in length or width, and need not be a working model, though it is preferable so to have it.

If the invention does not admit of illustration by model, or relates to some improvement
in chemistry or to a new process, a specimen of
the improved product should be furnished.

The model or specimen should be sent by express or brought to our office, unless another attorney is preferred.

In a separate letter should be sent, to the same address, a full description of the invention, pointing out its advantages, &c., and the first government fee of $15 inclosed therein, unless the applicant can call in person at the office. Should it appear that the invention is meritorious and a proper subject for a patent, the papers will be promptly prepared and submitted to the applicant for his approval, signature and oath, whereupon the usual attorney's fee of $25 will be due. After the papers are duly signed and sworn to, and the attorney's fee paid, the application is forwarded to the Patent Office and there examined.

If the patent is granted, the applicant is notified of the fact, and has to pay the second government fee of $20, within a reasonable time (six months), which payment insures the issue and delivery of the patent.

It will thus be seen, that the entire

COST OF A PATENT

is, if the invention is not too complicated, altogether, sixty dollars.

From these sixty dollars the Government

receives thirty-five, while the attorney's charge
for the preparation of the drawings and specifications and for attention to the prosecution of
the application is twenty-five dollars.

But if the invention is complicated and con-
sumes more than the average amount of time
and labor, in preparing drawings and papers,
the attorney's fee will be correspondingly increased.

The cost of the patent is thus, as follows :

First government fee................... $15
Attorney's fee, including cost of preparing
    drawings and specifications........... 25
Second government fee, payable when the
    patent is allowed.................... 20
                                  ——
                                $60

Thus, at an outlay of but sixty dollars, a patent may be obtained, which, if the invention is
meritorious, may yield a fortune.

There is certainly no safer and more profitable investment than a patent for a novel and
useful invention, nor one more easily accessible
to all classes of the people.

If an application for a patent is finally and
definitely rejected on the ground that the same
invention has been actually shown in some
former patent or printed publication, the appli-

cant will not have to pay the second government fee of $20, but he will forfeit the first government and the attorney's fee. When competent aid is solicited, the loss of these fees is very improbable, as it is generally, though not always, within the power of a zealous attorney to inform himself in advance of the actual state of the art to which the application intrusted to him belongs.

PROCEEDINGS IN WASHINGTON.

When an application for a patent reaches the United States Patent Office, the papers and model are first inspected, to ascertain whether they are executed and prepared in accordance with law and with the prescribed rules. If found to be correct, the inventor or his attorney is notified, that the application is duly filed, and that it will be examined in its order.

It is thereupon assigned to the examiner of that class of mechanics or chemistry, to which the invention pertains, as each examiner has a specific class under his supervision. When the examiner reaches the application in its order, he compares it carefully with patents, caveats, and publications embracing the same class of articles, to find whether the alleged invention has or has not been previously known.

If he finds the invention to be entirely new, and to be properly described, illustrated and claimed, he notifies the inventor (or his attorney) that the application has been examined and allowed, and that it will be passed for issue on receipt of the last Government fee of $20.

Upon receipt of this letter, or within six months from the date of same, the inventor may send to the attorney or the Patent Office, the said fee of $20, whereupon the patent will be issued and duly delivered to him.

˜ If, however, upon examination, the examiner finds that the alleged invention is anticipated in whole or in part, by previous publications, patents, or devices, he refers the inventor to such patents and rejects the application.

The inventor or his attorney may now compare his invention with the references cited by the examiner, and ascertain in what point, if any, it differs therefrom.

If he finds an important difference, he may point it out to the examiner, and pray for a reconsideration, or he may amend his application, so as to eliminate from it all that is shown to be old, and retain and claim the remaining new matter. The examiner will then, without additional cost, re-examine the application upon the argument or amendment submitted to him, and, if he is satisfied that the invention under consideration no longer interferes with other devices, will allow the patent. But if he still holds the application to be anticipated, he may again reject the application.

If the application has been twice rejected by the examiner upon the same ground, it is regarded as finally rejected, and the only remedy of the inventor to secure a patent is to

APPEAL.

Every applicant for a patent or the reissue of a patent, any of the claims of which have been twice rejected upon the same reference, may, if he should fail to agree with the primary examiner as to the propriety of the rejection, appeal from his decision to a Board of Examiners-in-chief. This board is composed of three examiners, specially selected for their superior legal and mechanical knowledge and attainments, and appointed to their office by the President of the United States. The Government fee for every such appeal is ten dollars.

The board looks carefully into the application, and considers in support thereof written or oral arguments of applicant's attorney, whereupon it will either reverse the primary examiner's decision or affirm the same. If the board reverses the decision the application will be allowed and the patent issued on payment of the second government fee; but if the board affirms the decision of the examiners, the inventors must, if he still deems his invention patentable, appeal to the Commissioner of Patents in person. The Government fee for this appeal is twenty dollars.

If the commissioner again rejects the application, an appeal may be taken to the Supreme Court of the District of Columbia, under special rules prescribed by said court.

Appeals in patent cases should not be carelessly prepared, as the experience of the examiners with inventions and with the rules of the Patent Office, and with the law as defined by said rules, is very extensive. The decisions of nearly all examiners should therefore be treated with respect, and are to some extent *prima facie* evidence of the matters set forth therein. That is to say, the invention is regarded as *not* patentable, if the examiner has so stated, and the applicant on appeal must assume the burden of proof to the contrary, before he can succeed in the application. The attorney's charge in appeal cases must therefore vary according to the nature of each case, and is necessarily a matter of special agreement.

MODELS.

Every invention which admits of illustration by a model should be embodied into one.

This model must not exceed one foot in length, and should be neat and tasteful in execution.

Wooden models should preferably be made of black walnut, or other handsome wood; metallic models of brass. It is best if the inventor can have his model made at home, but if this is not possible or practicable, we will recommend responsible model-makers upon application to that effect.

About one hundred and seventy-five thousand models of inventions are contained in the model-rooms of the United States Patent Office and there publicly exhibited.

A model is not only necessary to aid in the explanation of an inventions upon the filing of an application for a patent, but is very valuable after the patent has been granted in enabling the courts and the Patent Office to clearly interpret the scope of the patent in cases of legal controversy, or in applications for reissues or corrections of patents. And even after the expiration of a patent the model will be of value, in illustrating to the public the devices which it has a right to make, use and sell.

THE CENTENNIAL EXHIBITION.

The Commissioners' Report for the year 1876 contains the following :

" The display made at the Exposition by the Patent Office was creditable in every respect, and excited general attention. About 5,000 models of inventions, representing the leading branches of the arts and manufactures, were exhibited in suitable cases, and properly labeled, the various publications of the office were displayed, its practice fully explained to all inquirers, and copies of the patent laws and the office regulations and forms freely distributed.

" The knowledge of our patent system thus imparted to foreigners and all others, unable to visit Washington, has more than repaid the small cost attendant upon the representation.

" The exhibits were sent from and returned to the office with scarcely any damage being suffered.

" But the array of models &c., made by the Patent Office at the Exposition was not needed to illustrate the value of our patent practice. The wisdom of that system was demonstrated in the most practical and triumphant manner in nearly every branch of that munificent enterprise, not only in the grand display of labor-saving machinery, but in the vast collection of manufactured articles, and even in the department of fine arts were seen tho fruits of that provision in our Constitution, giving to Congress the power to promote the progress of science and the useful arts, by securing for limited times to authors and inventors, the exclusive right to their respective writings and discoveries."

A like gratifying result was achieved by the American inventors, who exhibited their devices in the Paris Exposition and carried away the principal prizes.

Whatever persons may do in an imaginary "perfect state of society" in sharing with others, without recompense, the fruits of their labor, it must be apparent that the wonderful growth of the useful arts in this country is thus far due to the protection given by our government to property in invention, a property as sacred as any other class of property, and whose value is usually determined like that of all other property, the product of human hands or brains, by the amount of veritable skill involved in its production.

GOING TO WASHINGTON.

Many inventors believe that by a personal visit to Washington, and by their attempts to *push* their appplications in the Patent Office, their interest will be improved. This expecta-

tion will hardly ever be realized. The routine
of the Patent Office is such that personal efforts
will, or at least should, count for nothing. The
object of engaging the services of a competent
attorney is not to gain time, for every case is
taken up in its turn, but to insure a proper representation of the case, both, when the same is
first submitted and also when it is to be prosecuted in the face of a rejection. The expense
which is connected with a trip to Washington
is therefore usually an absolute waste, as resort
to an attorney must, in nearly all cases, be
finally had before a patent can be issued.

REJECTED APPLICATIONS.

If an application, improperly conducted,
either by the inventor himself or by an incom-
petent agent, is rejected, although the invention is meritorious and should by right deserve
a patent, a copy of the application and of all
the proceedings before the Patent Office should
be sent to our office, together with a power
of attorney, to enable us to properly prosecute
the application and to present it in its true
light. We first give our opinion as to the propriety of proceeding further with such cases, and
always decline to take them in charge, unless
they present features of merit and of novelty.

The attorney's charge for prosecuting such applications is usually twenty-five dollars.

PRELIMINARY EXAMINATION.

Before applying for a patent a preliminary examination into the records of the Patent Office may be made, to ascertain whether the invention is probably new and patentable. Such an examination is usually ordered at the cost of only five dollars.

If an examination of this kind is desired, a brief description of the invention, together with the fee, should be remitted to us. We will then search and render a report, stating whether we consider the invention new or not.

In the latter case we give our reasons for the opinion.

These examinations are, however, owing to the comparatively superficial search which can be made for the small fee of five dollars, not absolutely reliable, and do not extend into foreign patents or publications. They are confined to American patents; but more extensive searches can, of course, be made for a correspondingly increased fee, which parties engaged in *important* enterprises are usually willing to invest, provided they have reason to believe that the attorney will return honest effort for their money.

ASSIGNMENTS.

Every invention can, by its inventor, be assigned in whole or in part to others, before or after the issue of the patent. It is a matter of every day occurrence that an inventor, if his means do not suffice, assigns to another a share such as one-half, one-third, or the like, of his invention and of a patent that may be granted therefor, so as thus to obtain the means necessary for preparing a model and securing a patent, perhaps also for starting a new manufacture under the patent.

Assignments and agreements relating to patents will be carefully prepared at our office.

The cost of an ordinary assignment, including the fee for recording it in the Patent Office, is five dollars.

The cost of an agreement differs with its length and with the importance of the matter involved, as the responsibility of the attorney increases in corresponding degree. All assignments of inventions or patents should be recorded within three months after the dates of their execution.

If the assignment is executed and recorded before the patent is allowed, or, in fact, at any time before the second Government fee of $20 is paid, the patent will issue to the assignee.

Before executing any assignment the inventor

should always consult a competent attorney, who will guard him against the commission of errors which have proved fatal to many, who were over-confident in their own knowledge of the Patent Law.

A DESIGN PATENT

is granted to any person, whether a citizen or alien, who, by his own industry, genius, efforts and expense, has invented or produced a new and original design for a manufacture, bust, statue, alto-relievo, a bas-relief, any new and original design for the printing of woolen, silk, cotton, or other fabrics; any new and original impression, ornament, pattern, print, or picture to be printed, painted, cast, or otherwise placed on or worked into any article of manufacture, or in short any new or original shape or configuration of any article of manufacture.

A design patent, in contradistinction to a mechanical patent, is granted for the new ornamentation, pattern or shape of an article, and not for its mechanical merits.

Such patents are frequently taken for new carpet-patterns, lace fabrics, for ornamental castings, glassware, and the like, to prevent the imitation of the new designs embodied therein.

A design patent is granted for the term of 3½,

7 or 14 years, as the applicant may elect. The Government fee for a 3½ years' design patent is $10; for a 7 years' design patent, $15, and for a 14 years' design patent, $30.

The attorney's fee is usually $15, unless drawings of the designs have first to be made, which may render the application more costly. Usually, however, the entire cost of a design patent is either $25, $30 or $45, according to the length of time for which it is taken.

When the design can be sufficiently represented by photographic illustrations, twelve such photographs should be furnished, or the article itself may be sent to our office, so that we may have proper drawings prepared.

To apply for a design patent, a model, drawing or photograph of the invention should be furnished to the attorney, together with the fees above mentioned. We will then proceed as with an application for a mechanical patent.

RE-ISSUES.

A re-issue is granted to the original patentee (or to his legal representatives, if the inventor is dead), or to his assignees, when by reason of a defective or insufficient specification in the original patent, the same is inoperative or invalid or does not secure to the owner the full

protection which the invention should receive.
The old patent will, in that case, be canceled
by the Patent Office and a new and revised
patent for the same invention issued for the
unexpired term of the original patent. The
government fee for a re-issue is $30, payable in
advance; the attorney's charge usually $30,
making the entire cost $60.

In order to obtain a re-issue the original patent should be remitted to our office, together
with the fee, and with a statement, showing in
what particulars the patent is regarded defective.
If we agree to take charge of the case, we will
have the papers properly prepared and remitted
to the applicant for approval and signature;
whereupon the application is forwarded to
Washington, together with the old patent. If
the re-issue is refused, the old patent will be returned. If, however, the re-issue is granted, the
old patent is cancelled.

In cases where more than one invention is
included in one patent, re-issues thereof may be
taken in several divisions, in which case every
division will constitute a new and complete
patent. The cost of each division is equal to
that of a single re-issue. Before suits for in-
fringements of patents are commenced, it is
usually advisable to request a competent attor-

ney to carefully scrutinize the patent to ascertain whether it is defective, and to correct any defects he may discover, by re-issue, as otherwise the suits may be lost owing to informalities in the patents upon which they are based.

CAVEATS.

A caveat is a limited protection whereby during one year the inventor is entitled to receive official notice of every application which may be filed by others, during said year, for a patent for the same invention as that described in the caveat. A caveat is usually filed while an inventor is still experimenting on his invention, and before he has the same in proper shape to apply for a patent, and its object is to prevent other parties, pending such experiments, from obtaining a patent for the same invention. If, during the year, another person applies for a patent with which such caveat would in any manner conflict, the application will be suspended and notice thereof sent to the caveator, who, if he shall file a complete application within three months after receiving the notice, will be entitled to an interference with the previous application for the purpose of proving priority of invention, and obtaining the patent if he be adjudged the first inventor. A caveat can only be filed by a citizen of the United States, or by a foreigner who has resided in the United States at least one year previous to the application, and has declared his intention of becoming a citizen.

The government fee for filing a caveat is $10 ; the attorney's fee usually $15, making the total cost of a caveat $25. For filing a caveat a description and sketch of the invention should be furnished and remitted with the fee to our office, 258 Broadway, New York.

TRADE MARKS.

A trade mark is a name, sign or symbol adopted by corporations, firms, or persons in business, to distinguish their goods from goods of the same class, but of other manufacturers or dealers.

Trade marks can be registered in the United States Patent Office, and will thereby be brought under the jurisdiction of the United States courts, to facilitate the prosecution of imitators, and prevent the publication of counterfeits of the registered marks by unauthorized parties.

Trade marks properly registered afford a very powerful protection to their owners, and should be registered by all parties whose business is of sufficient importance to warrant the outlay connected with the registration.

The law of August 14, 1876, provides that every person who shall, with intent to defraud, deal in, or sell, or keep goods of substantially the same descriptive properties as those referred to in the registration of a trade mark, to which a fraudulent imitation of said trade mark is affixed, shall be punished by a fine not exceeding one thousand dollars or imprisoned not more than two years, or both such fine and imprisonment.

It will thus be seen that the courts are authorized to extend powerful protection to the owners of trade marks and severely to punish counterfeiters.

As many as nine hundred and fifty-nine trademarks were registered during the year 1876; over fourteen hundred in 1878. A trade mark can only be registered by a person or firm domiciled in the United Sates, or by a corporation created by the authority of the United States, or of any State or Territory thereof, or by any person, firm, or corporation resident of or located in any foreign country, which by treaty or convention affords a similar privilege to citizens of the United States. Thus far, these countries are England, Germany, France, Russia, Belgium and Austria.

The government fee for registering a trade mark is $25; the attorney's fee, usually $15. In order to register a trade mark, twelve copies of the mark, together with a statement containing the names of the members of the firm, their places of residence and the citizenship of each member; also the length of time for which the trade mark has been used, and the class of goods to which it is applied, should be furnished us, together with the fee of $40. The papers will then be properly prepared and forwarded for signature, and afterward submitted to the Patent Office. After the registration of a trade-mark has been allowed, a certificate setting forth the facts relating to the registration and accompanied by a copy of the trade mark, under the seal of the Patent Office, will be delivered to the applicant. By a new rule of the Patent Office, the fee for registering a trade mark may be paid in two installments, viz., $10 upon filing the application, and $15 after the same has been allowed.

LABELS AND PRINTS.

Labels and prints which are applied to goods and merchandise to designate their quality, etc., *and which do not contain a trade mark*, may be registered under the copyright law in the

United States Patent Office. The government fee for such registration is $6, and the attorney's fee usually $9, together $15, which should be paid on making the application.

For registering a label or print, seven copies thereof should be sent to our office, together with the fee, whereupon the papers will be duly prepared.

Printers, lithographers and designers of new labels or prints can register the same as such, and will find it to their advantage so to do, in order to avoid imitation by other printers. But dealers in articles of manufacture will derive little benefit from such registration, their protection being under the law relating to *trade marks*, not under the copyright law.

COPYRIGHTS.

Any citizen of the United States or resident therein who is the author, designer or proprietor of a new book, map, chart, musical composition, engraving, drawing, statue or other work of art, may obtain a copyright for the same, in order to prevent others from imitating his production. Copyrights are of importance to dramatists, musical composers, authors, and artists, as they insure to them the exclusive right to reproduce their productions. In fact, were it not for the Copyright Laws, no author in the United States could prevent others in this country from copying and reproducing his works as soon as published, and it would be a very unprofitable business to waste time in the production of a new work which could be published and reproduced by others, who did not share the effort of its production. It is, therefore, to the Copyright Laws, that we are said to be indebted for the growth of literature and the fine arts in this country. If this growth is not in keeping with the expectations of the people, it is due principally to the very narrow-minded policy, embodied in the same law, of excluding foreigners from the enjoyment of a copyright in the United States. Consequence is, that American publishers may and do copy the best products of English literature, *without paying any compensation to their authors*, and that they are consequently unwilling to publish works of American origin, on which royalties would have to be paid. Thus the American author is discouraged, and a system, which was intended to foster home-industry, is a most effective means of suppressing home development of fine arts and literature. Redress for this evil can only be expected when Congress shall pay less deference to wealthy book-sellers than to the true welfare of the nation.

Copyrights are registered by the Librarian of Congress, and are granted for the term of twenty-eight years, which may be extended for fourteen more years.

In order to secure a copyright, a printed copy of the title of the book or other article to be copyrighted, or a description of the painting, drawing, statue, or design for a work of the fine arts, for which the copyright is desired, must be sent to the Librarian of Congress before publication, and within ten days from the publication, two copies of such book, or of the photograph of the painting, drawing, statue or design, must also be forwarded.

Through our establishment a number of copyrights has been secured.

The fee in each case is six dollars, which includes the Government fee of $1, and should be forwarded to us, together with a copy of the title or a description of the work to be copyrighted, and with the name or names of the owners. The case will then be duly attended to. After publication, the two copies or photographs of the article to be copyrighted, should also be sent to us.

Copyrights are assignable by an instrument of

writing; such assignment must be recorded in the office of the Librarian of Congress within sixty days after its execution, in default of which it is void against any subsequent purchaser or mortgagee for a valuable consideration without notice.

Our charge for drawing and recording a copyright assignment is usually five dollars; this fee may, however, vary according to the circumstances of each case.

FOREIGN PATENTS.

American inventions are much sought after in Canada, England, France, Germany, Belgium and other foreign countries, and patentees frequently realize large profits from patents for their inventions in these countries.

A Canadian patent will prevent the imitation of the invention in the neighboring Provinces. We are, by good connections in London, Berlin, Paris, Vienna, Madrid and Montreal, prepared to make applications for patents in all foreign countries, and to properly represent the interests of the inventors as far as securing their patents in foreign countries is concerned.

The rates of foreign patents will be furnished upon special inquiry at our office, No. 258 Broadway, New York.

As English, German and Spanish patents are

granted to the first *introducers*, to the exclusion of the first inventors, it will be to the interest of the true inventor to apply for the English, German and Spanish patent before the American patent is *issued* and *published;* otherwise, the publication of the United States patent in the Official Gazette may invalidate the English as well as the German or Spanish patent subsequently obtained.

The taking out of a patent in a foreign country does not prejudice a patent previously obtained here ; nor does it prevent the obtainment of a patent here, subsequent to the foreign patent, unless the invention shall have been introduced into public use in the United States for more than two years prior to the application. But when a patent is taken out in this country for an invention previously patented abroad, the American patent will expire at the same time with the foreign patent, or, if there be more than one, at the same time with the one having the shortest term. The best course which an inventor can pursue, therefore, who wishes to obtain patents in this and in foreign countries, is to apply for the United States patent first, and after the same has been allowed, *but before it is issued,* to apply for the foreign patents.

INTERFERENCE CASES.

When two or more parties have applications for patents for the *same* invention pending before the Patent Office at the same time, or when an applicant, having been rejected upon any unexpired patent, claims to have made the invention before the patentee, *an interference* will be declared in order to ascertain who is the first and original inventor of the matter in controversy. An interference is, therefore, a proceeding before the Patent Office, instituted for the purpose of determining the question of *priority of invention* between two or more parties who claim the same patentable subject matter. Interference suits must be very carefully conducted, and usually require the services of skilled and experienced attorneys. It frequently happens that different parties have made the same invention, at nearly the same time, or that a party applies for a patent for an article which he has seen another person construct or invent, and which, nevertheless, he fraudulently seeks to appropriate to himself. It is in such cases a matter of great difficulty to ascertain and prove to the Patent Office who is the prior and true inventor, and who the mere imitator.

Interference cases should therefore be intrusted only to trustworthy attorneys.

The proceedings in an interference case are as follows:

Before the declaration of an interference, the issue must be clearly defined, the invention must be decided to be patentable, and the application put in such condition as to require no subsequent alterations.

Each party will thereupon be required to file a brief statement under oath, showing the date of the original conception by him of the subject matter in controversy, the date of its completion, and other details pertaining to the history of the invention. These statements are sealed and sent to the Patent Office, where they are opened by the Examiner of Interferences, who thereupon declares the interference proper, and orders the several parties thereto to examine witnesses and take other proofs, in order to show and prove to the Patent Office the truthfulness of the preliminary statements filed by them. After all the proofs have been duly taken, a hearing is had in Washington before the Examiner of Interferences, at which the attorneys for the parties are allowed to speak, and their arguments in favor of their clients will be received. Thereupon and after carefully considering the testimony and the arguments of the various parties, the Examiner of Interferences renders his decision in favor of the party whom he believes the first and original inventor of the subject matter in controversy.

Two appeals may be taken from his decision by the party or parties against whom the decision is rendered, one to the Board of Examiners in chief, and another to the Commissioner of Patents in person.

The party who is finally adjudged to be the true inventor of the subject matter involved, will be entitled to and will receive the patent.

Various well established rules govern the manner in which the testimony is to be taken, and the proceedings, in case one party fails to file a preliminary statement, or to take any testimony whatsoever, all of which can only be ascertained by experience and practice.

The cost of interference suits differs, of course, with the amount of testimony and with the labor involved in the case. Sometimes, when parties have a clear and strong case, it is not necessary to take much testimony; but frequently a large amount of proofs must be taken.

Parties who are thrown into interference controversies should submit their cases to us *before* filing their preliminary statements, as the propriety of the interference cannot be questioned after the filing of said statements, and also because the preparation of the preliminary statement itself requires careful study, the parties being bound thereto in their proofs subsequently taken.

AN INFRINGEMENT SUIT

is brought in the United States Court by the owner of a patent in order to restrain others from infringing upon his patent, and from fraudulently imitating the patented articles. The patentee, if he proves his case, will be entitled to collect from the infringer the costs of the suit and the damages sustained by the infringement, or the profits made by the infringer, or both damages and profits; he will also be entitled to an injunction against the imitator.

As infringement suits are usually of great importance, and involve large interests, it is necessary to select proper counsel for conducting these suits.

Further information may be obtained by addressing or calling at our office, 258 Broadway, New York.

All communications strictly confidential.

A. v. BRIESEN,
Attorney in Patent Cases.

THE PATENT LAW.

SECTION 4883. All patents shall be issued in the name of the United States of America, under the seal of the Patent Office, and shall be signed by the Secretary of the Interior and countersigned by the Commissioner of Patents, and they shall be recorded, together with the specifications, in the Patent Office, in books to be kept for that purpose.

SEC. 4884. Every patent shall contain a short title or description of the invention or discovery, correctly indicating its nature and design, and a grant to the patentee, his heirs or assigns, for the term of seventeen years, of the exclusive right to make, use and vend the invention or discovery throughout the United States, and the Territories thereof, referring to the specification for the particulars thereof. A copy of the specification and drawings shall be annexed to the patent and be a part thereof.

SEC. 4885. Every patent shall bear date as of a day not later than six months from the time at which it was passed and allowed and notice thereof was sent to the applicant or his agent ; and if the final fee is not paid within that period the patent shall be withheld.

SEC. 4886. Any person who has invented or discovered any new and useful art, machine, manufacture or composition of matter, or any new and useful improvement thereof, not known nor used by others in this country, and not patented or described in any printed publication in this or any foreign country, before his invention or discovery thereof, and not in public use or on sale for more than two years prior to his application, unless the same is proved to have been abandoned, may upon payment of the fees required by law, and other due proceedings had, obtain a patent therefor.

SEC. 4887. No person shall be debarred from receiving a patent for his invention or discovery, nor shall any patent be declared invalid, by reason of its having been first patented or caused to be patented in a foreign country, unless the same has been introduced into public use in the United States for more than two years prior to the application. But every patent granted for an invention which has been previously patented in a foreign country shall be so limited as to expire at the same time with the foreign patent, or, if there be more than one, at the same time with the one having the shortest term, and in no case shall it be in force more than seventeen years.

SEC. 4888. Before any inventor or discoverer shall receive a patent for his invention or discovery, he shall make application therefor, in writing, to the Commissioner of Patents, and shall file in the Patent Office a written description of the same, and of the manner aud process of making, constructing, compounding, and using it, in such full, clear, concise, and exact terms as to enable any person skilled in the art or science to which it appertains, or with which it is most nearly connected, to make, construct, compound, and use the same ; and in case of a machine, he shall explain the principle thereof, and the best mode in which he has contemplated applying that principle, so as to distinguish it from other inventions ; and he shall particularly point out and distinctly claim the part, improvement, or combination which he claims as his invention or discovery. The specification and claim shall be signed by the inventor and attested by two witnesses.

SEC. 4889. When the nature of the case admits of drawings, the applicant shall furnish one copy signed by the inventor or his attorney in fact and attested by two witnesses, which shall be filed in the Patent Office ; and a copy of the drawing, to be furnished by the Patent Office, shall be attached to the patent as a part of the specification.

SEC. 4890. When the invention or discovery is of a composition of matter, the applicant, if required by the Commissioner, shall furnish specimens of ingredients and of the composition, sufficient in quantity for the purpose of experiment.

SEC. 4891. In all cases which admit of representation by model, the applicant, if required by the Commissioner, shall furnish a model of convenient size to exhibit advantageously the several parts of his invention or discovery.

SEC. 4892. The applicant shall make oath that he does verily believe himself to be the original and first inventor or discoverer of the art, machine, manufacture, composition, or improvement for which he solicits a patent ; that he does not know and does not believe that the same was ever before known or used ; and shall state of what country he is a citizen. Such oath may be made before any person within the United States authorized by law to administer oaths, or when the applicant resides in a foreign country, before any minister, charge d'affaires, consul, or commercial agent, holding commission under the Government of the United States, or before any notary public of the foreign country in which the applicant may be.

SEC. 4893. On the filing of any such application and the payment of the fees required by law, the Commissioner of Patents shall cause an examination to be made of the alleged new invention or discovery ; and if on such examination it shall appear that the claimant is justly entitled to a patent under the law, and that the same is sufficiently useful and important, the Commissioner shall issue a patent therefor.

SEC. 4894. All applications for patents shall be completed and prepared for examination within two years after the filing of the application, and in default thereof, or upon failure of the applicant to prosecute the same within two years after any action therein, of which notice shall have been given to the applicant, they shall be regarded as abandoned by the parties thereto, unless it be shown to the satisfaction of the Commissioner of Patents that such delay was unavoidable.

SEC. 4895. Patents may be granted and issued or reissued to the assignee of the inventor or discoverer ; but the assignment must first be entered of record in the Patent Office. And in all cases of an application by an assignee for the issue of a patent, the application shall be made and the specification sworn to by the inventor or discoverer; and in all cases of an application for a reissue of any patent, the application must be made and the corrected specification signed by the inventor or discoverer, if he is living, unless the patent was issued and the assignment made before the eighth day of July, eighteen hundred and seventy.

SEC. 4896. When any person, having made any new invention or discovery for which a patent might have been granted, dies before a patent is granted, the right of applying for and obtaining the patent shall devolve on his executor or administrator, in trust for the heirs at law of the deceased, in case he shall have died intestate ; or if he shall have left a will disposing of the same, then in trust for his devisees, in as full manner and on the same terms and conditions as the same might have been claimed or enjoyed by him in his lifetime; and when the application is made by such legal representatives, the oath or affirmation required to be made shall be so varied in form that it can be made by them.

SEC. 4897. Any person who has an interest in an invention or discovery, whether as inventor, discoverer, or assignee, for which a patent was ordered to issue upon the payment of the final fee, but who fails to make payment thereof within six months from the time at which it was passed and allowed, and notice thereof was sent to the applicant or his agent, shall have a right to make an application for a patent for such invention or discovery the same as in the case of an original application. But such second application must be made within two years after the allowance of the original application. But no person shall be held responsible in damages for the manufacture or use of any article or thing for which a patent was ordered to issue under such renewed application prior to the issue of the patent. And upon the hearing of renewed applications preferred under this section, abandonment shall be considered as a question of fact.

SEC. 4898. Every patent or any interest therein shall be assignable in law by an instrument in writing; and the patentee or his assigns or legal representatives may, in like manner, grant and convey an exclusive right under his patent to the whole or any specified part of the United States. An assignment, grant, or conveyance shall be void as against any subsequent purchaser or mortgagee for a valuable consideration, without notice, unless it is recorded in the Patent Office within three months from the date thereof.

SEC. 4899. Every person who purchases of the inventor or discoverer, or with his knowledge and consent constructs any newly invented or discovered machine, or other patentable article, prior to the application by the inventor or discoverer for a patent, or who sells or uses one so constructed, shall have the right to use, and vend to others to be used, the specific thing so made or purchased, without liability therefor.

SEC. 4900. It shall be the duty of all patentees, and their assigns and legal representatives, and of all persons making or vending any patented article for or under them, to give sufficient notice to the public that the same is patented, either by fixing thereon the word "patented," together with the day and year the patent was granted, or when, from the character of the article, this cannot be done, by fixing to it, or to the package wherein one or more of them is inclosed a label containing the like notice ; and in any suit for infringement by the party failing so to mark, no damages shall be recovered by the plaintiff, except on proof that the defendant was duly notified of the infringement, and continued, after such notice, to make, use or vend the article so patented.

SEC. 4901. Every person who, in any manner, marks upon anything made, used, or sold by him for which he has not obtained a patent, the name or any imitation of the name of any person who has obtained a patent therefor, without the consent of such patentee or his assigns or legal representatives ; or

Who, in any manner, marks upon or affixes to any such patented article the word "patent" or "patentee," or the words "letters-patent," or any word of like import, with intent to imitate or counterfeit the mark or device of the patentee, without having the license or consent of such patentee or his assigns or legal representatives ; or

Who, in any manner, marks upon or affixes to any unpatented article the word "patent" or any word importing that the same is patented, for the purpose of deceiving the public, shall be liable, for every such offense, to a penalty of not less than one hundred dollars, with costs; one half said penaly to the person who shall sue for the same, and the other to the use of the United States, to be recovered by suit in any District Court of the United States within whose jurisdiction such offense may have been committed.

SEC. 4902. Any citizen of the United States who makes any new invention or discovery, and desires further time to mature the same, may, on payment of the fees reqnired by law, file in the Patent Office a caveat setting forth the design thereof, and of its distinguishing characteristics, and praying protection of his right until he shall have matured his invention. Such caveat shall be filed in the confidential archives of the office and preserved in secrecy, and shall be operative for the term of one year from the filing thereof; and if application is made within the year by any other person for a patent with which such caveat would in any manner interfere, the Commissioner shall deposit the description, specification, drawings, and model of such application in like manner in the confidential archives of the office, and give notice thereof, by mail, to the person by whom the caveat was filed. If such person desires to avail himself of his caveat, he shall file his description, specifications, drawings, and model within three months from the time of placing the notice in the Post-office in Washington, with the usual time required for transmitting it to the caveator added thereto; which time shall be indorsed on the notice. An alien shall have the privilege herein granted, if he has resided in the United States one year next preceding the filing of his caveat, and has made oath of his intention to become a citizen.

SEC. 4903. Whenever, on examination, any claim for a patent is rejected, the Commissioner shall notify the applicant thereof, giving him briefly the reasons for such rejection, together with such information and references as may be useful in judging of the propriety of renewing his application or of altering his specification ; and if, after receiving such notice, the applicant persists in his claim for a patent, with or without altering his specifications, the Commissioner shall order a re-examination of the case.

Sec. 4904. Whenever an application is made for a patent which, in the opinion of the Commissioner, would interfere with any pending application, or with any unexpired patent, he shall give notice thereof to the applicants, or applicant and patentee, as the case may be, and shall direct the primary examiner to proceed to determine the question of priority of invention. And the Commissioner may issue a patent to the party who is adjudged the prior inventor, unless the adverse party appeals from the decision of the primary examiner, or of the Board of Examiners-in-chief, as the case may be, within such time, not less than twenty days, as the Commissioner shall prescribe.

Sec. 4905. The Commissioner of Patents may establish rules for taking affidavits and depositions required in cases pending in the Patent Office, and such affidavits and depositions may be taken before any officer authorized by law to take depositions to be used in the courts of the United States, or of the State where the officer resides.

Sec. 4906. The Clerk of any court of the United States, for any district or Territory where'n testimony is to be taken for use in any contested case pending in the Patent Office, shall, upon the application of any party thereto, or of his agent or attorney, issue a subpœna for any witness residing or being within such disirict or Territory, commanding him to appear and testify before any officer in such district or Territory authorized to take depositions and affidavits, at any time and place in the subpœna stated. But no witness shall be required to attend at any place more than forty miles from the place where the subpœna is served upon him.

Sec. 4907. Every witness duly subpœnaed and in attendance shall be allowed the same fees as are allowed to witnesses attending the courts of the United States.

Sec. 4908. Whenever any witness, after being duly served with such subpœna, neglects or refuses to appear, or after appearing refuses to testify, the judge of the court whose clerk issued the subpœna may, on proof of such neglect or refusal, enforce obedience to the process, or punish the disobedience, as in other like cases. But no witness shall be guilty of contempt for disobeying such subpœna unless his fees and traveling expenses in going to, returning from, and one day's attendance at the place of examination, are paid or tendered him at the time of the service of the subpœna; nor for refusing to disclose any secret invention or discovery made or owned by himself.

Sec. 4909. Every applicant for a patent or for the reissue for a patent, any of the claims of which have been twice rejected, and every party to an interference, may appeal from the decision of the primary examiner, or of the examiner in charge of interferences in such case, to the Board of Examiners-in-chief, having once paid the fee for such appeal.

SEC. 4910. If such party is dissatisfied with the decision of the Examiners-in-chief, he may, on payment of the fee prescribed, appeal to the Commissioner in person.

SEC. 4911. If such party, except a party to an interference, is dissatisfied with the decision of the Commissioner, he may appeal to the Supreme Court of the District of Columbia, sitting in banc.

SEC. 4912. When an appeal is taken to the Supreme Court of the District of Columbia, the appellant shall give notice thereof to the Commissioner, and file in the Patent Office, within such time as the Commissioner shall appoint, his reasons of appeal, specifically set forth in writing.

SEC. 4913. The court shall, before hearing such appeal, give notice to the Commissioner of the time and place of the hearing, and on receiving such notice the Commissioner shall give notice of such time and place in such manner as the court may prescribe, to all parties who appear to be interested therein. The party appealing shall lay before the court certified copies of all the original papers and evidence in the case, and the Commissioner shall furnish the court with the grounds of his decision, fully set forth in writing, touching all the points involved by the reasons of appeal. And at the request of any party interested, or of the court, the Commissioner and the examiners may be examined under oath, in explanation of the principles of the thing for which a patent is demanded.

SEC. 4914. The court, on petition, shall hear and determine such appeal, and revise the decision appealed from in a summary way, on the evidence produced before the Commissioner, at such early and convenient time as the court may appoint ; and the revision shall be confined to the points set forth in the reasons of appeal. After hearing the case the court shall return to the Commissioner a certificate of its proceedings and decision, which shall be entered of record in the Patent Office, and shall govern the further proceedings in the case. But no opinion or decision of the court in any such case shall preclude any person interested from the right to contest the validity of such patent in any court wherein the same may be called in question.

SEC. 4915. Whenever a patent on application is refused, either by the Commissioner of Patents or by the Supreme Court of the District of Columbia upon appeal from the Commissioner, the applicant may have remedy by bill in equity; and the court having cognizance thereof, on notice to adverse parties and other due proceedings had, may adjudge that such applicant is entitled, according to law, to receive a patent for his invention, as specified in his claim, or for any part thereof, as the facts in the case may appear. And such adjudication, if it be in favor of the right of the applicant, shall authorize the Commissioner to issue such patent on the applicant filing in the Patent Office a copy of the adjudication, and otherwise complying with the requirements of law. In all cases, where there is no opposing party, a copy of the bill shall be served on the Commissioner; and all the expenses of the proceedings shall be paid by the applicant, whether the final decision is in his favor or not.

Sec. 4916. Whenever any patent is inoperative or invalid, by reason of a defective or insufficient specification, or by reason of the patentee claiming as his own invention or discovery more than he had a right to claim as new, if the error has arisen by inadvertence, accident, or mistake, and without any fraudulent or deceptive intention, the Commissioner shall, on the surrender of such patent and the payment of the duty required by law, cause a new patent for the same invention, and in accordance with the corrected specification, to be issued to the patentee, or, in the case of his death or of an assignment of the whole or any undivided part of the original patent, then to his executors, administrators, or assigns, for the unexpired part of the term of the original patent. Such surrender shall take effect upon the issue of the amended patent. The Commissioner may, in his discretion, cause several patents to be issued for distinct and separate parts of the thing patented, upon demand of the applicant, and upon payment of the required fee for a reissue for each of such reissued letters patent. The specifications and claim in every such case shall be subject to revision and restriction in the same manner as original applications are. Every patent so reissued, together with the corrected specification, shall have the same effect and operation in law, on the trial of all actions for causes thereafter arising, as if the same had been originally filed in such corrected form ; but no new matter shall be introduced into the specification, nor in case of a machine patent shall the model or drawings be amended, except each by the other; but when there is neither model nor drawing, amendments may be made upon proof satisfactory to the Commissioner that such new matter or amendment was a part of the original invention, and was omitted from the specification by inadvertence, accident, or mistake, as aforesaid.

Sec. 4917. Whenever, through inadvertence, accident, or mistake, and without any fraudulent or deceptive intention, a patentee has claimed more than that of which he was the original or first inventor or discoverer, his patent shall be valid for all that part which is truly and justly his own, provided the same is a material or substantial part of the thing patented; and any such patentee, his heirs or assigns, whether of the whole or any sectional interest therein, may on payment of the fee required by law, make disclaimer of such parts of the thing patented as he shall not choose to claim or to hold by virtue of the patent or assignment, stating therein the extent of his interest in such patent. Such disclaimer shall be in writing, attested by one or more witnesses, and recorded in the Patent Office; and it shall thereafter be considered as part of the original specification to the extent of the interest possessed by the claimant and by those claiming under him after the record thereof. But no such disclaimer shall affect any action pending at the time of its being filed, except so far as may relate to the question of unreasonable neglect or delay in filing it.

Sec. 4918. Whenever there are interfering patents, any person interested in any one of them, or in the working of the invention claimed under either of them, may have relief against the interfering patentee, and all parties interested under him, by suit in equity against the owners of the interfering patent; and the court, on notice to adverse parties, and other due proceedings had according to the course of equity, may adjudge and declare either of the patents void in whole or in part, or inoperative, or invalid in any particular part of the United States, according to the interest of the parties in the patent or the invention patented. But no such judgment or adjudication shall affect the right of any person except the parties to the suit and those deriving title under them subsequent to the rendition of such judgment.

SEC. 4819. Damages for the infringement of any patent may be recovered by action on the case, in the name of the party interested, either as patentee, assignee, or grantee. And whenever in any such action a verdict is rendered for the plaintiff, the court may enter judgment thereon for any sum above the amount found by the verdict as the actual damage sustained, according to the circumstances of the case. not exceeding three times the amount of such verdict, together with the costs.

SEC. 4920. In any action for infringement the defendant may plead the general issue, and having given notice in writing to the plaintiff or his attorney thirty days before, may prove, on trial, any one or more of the following special matters·

First.—That for the purpose of deceiving the public, the description and specification filed by the patentee in the Patent Office was made to contain less than the whole truth relative to his invention or discovery, or more than is necessary to produce the desired effect; or,

Second.—That he had surreptitiously or unjustly obtained the patent for that which was in fact invented by another, who was using reasonable diligence in adapting and perfecting the same; or,

T ird.—That it had been patented or described in some printed publication prior to his supposed invention or discovery thereof; or

Fourth.—That he was not the original and first inventor or discoverer of any material and substantial part of the thing patented; or,

Fifth.—That it had been in public use or on sale in this country for more than two years before his application for a patent, or had been abandoned to the public.

And in notices as to proof of previous invention, knowledge, or use of the thing patented, the defendant shall state the names of patentees and the dates of their patents, and when granted, and the names and residences of the persons alleged to have invented, or to have had the prior knowledge of the thing patented, and where and by whom it had been used; and if any one or more of the special matters alleged shall be found for the defendant, judgment shall be rendered for him with costs. And the like defenses may be pleaded in any suit in equity for relief against an alleged infringement; and proofs of the same may be given upon like notice in the answer of the defendant, and with the like effect.

SEC. 4921. The several courts vested with jurisdiction of cases arising under the patent laws shall have power to grant injunctions according to the course and principles of courts of equity, to prevent the violation of any right secured by patent, on such terms as the court may deem reasonable; and upon a decree being rendered in any such case for an infringement, the complainant shall be entitled to recover, in addition to the profits to be accounted for by the defendant, the damages the complainant has sustained thereby; and the court shall assess the same or cause the same to be assessed under its direction. And the court shall have the same power to increase such damages, in its discretion, as is given to increase the damages found by verdicts in actions in the nature of actions of trespass upon the case.

SEC. 4922. Whenever, through inadvertence, accident, or mistake, and without any willful default or intent to defraud or mislead the public, a patentee has, in his specification, claimed to be the original and first inventor or discoverer of any material or substantial part of the thing patented, of which he was not the original and first inventor or discoverer, every such patentee, his executors, administrators, and assigns, whether of the whole or any sectional interest in the patent, may maintain a suit at law or in equity for the infringement of any part thereof which was *bona fide* his own, if it is a material and substantial part of the thing patented, and definitely distinguishable from the parts claimed without right, notwithstanding the specifications may embrace more than that of which the patentee was the first inventor or discoverer. But in every such case in which a judgment or decree shall be rendered for the plaintiff no costs shall be recovered unless the proper disclaimer has been entered at the Patent Office before the commencement of the suit. But no patentee shall be entitled to the benefits of this section if he has unreasonably neglected or delayed to enter a disclaimer.

SEC. 4923. Whenever it appears that a patentee, at the time of making his application for the patent, believed himself to be the original and first inventor or discoverer of the thing patented, the same shall not be held to be void on account of the invention or discovery, or any part thereof, having been known or used in a foreign country, before his invention or discovery thereof, if it had not been patented or described in a printed publication.

SEC. 4924, 4925, 4926 and 4927 relate to the manner of extending Patents that expired before March 2, 1875.

SEC. 4928. The benefit of the extension of a patent shall extend to the assignees and grantees of the right to use the thing patented, to the extent of their interest therein.

DESIGNS.

SEC. 4929. Any person who by his own industry, genius, efforts, and expense, has invented and produced any new and original design for a manufacture, bust, statue, alto-relievo, or bas-relief: any new and original design for the printing of woolen, silk, cotton, or other fabrics; any new and original impression, ornament, patent [pattern], print, or picture to be printed, painted, cast, or otherwise placed on or worked into any article of manufacture; or any new, useful, and original shape or configuration of any article of manufacture, the same not having been known or used by others before his invention or production thereof, or patented or described in any printed publication, may, upon payment of the fee prescribed, and other due proceedings had, the same as in cases of inventions or discoveries, obtain a patent therefor.

SEC. 4930. The Commissioner may dispense with models of designs when the design can be sufficiently represented by drawings or photographs.

SEC. 4931. Patents for designs may be granted for the term of three years and six months, or for seven years, or for fourteen years, as the applicant may, in his application, elect.

SEC. 4932. Patentees of designs issued prior to the second day of March, eighteen hundred and sixty-one, shall be entitled to extension of their respective patents for the term of seven years, in the same manner and under the same restrictions as are provided for the extension of patents for inventions or discoveries, issued prior to the second day of March, eighteen hundred and sixty-one.

SEC. 4933. All the regulations and provisions which apply to obtaining or protecting patents for inventions or discoveries not incon sistent with the provisions of this Title, shall apply to patents for designs.

FEES.

SEC. 4934. The following shall be the rates for patent fees:

On filing each original application for a patent; except in design cases, fifteen dollars.

On issuing each original patent, except in design cases, twenty dollars.

In design cases; For three years and six months, ten dollars ; for seven years, fifteen dollars ; for fourteen years; thirty dollars.

On filing each caveat, ten dollars.

On every application for the reissue of a patent, thirty dollars.

On filing each disclaimer, ten dollars.

On every application for the extension of a patent, fifty dollars.

On the granting of every extension of a patent, fifty dollars.

On an appeal for the first time from the primary examiners to the examiners-in-chief, ten dollars.

On every appeal from the examiners-in-chief to the Commissioner, twenty dollars.

For certified copies of patents and other papers, including certified printed copies, ten cents per hundred words.

For recording every assignment, agreement, power of attorney, or other paper, of three hundred words or under, one dollar; of over three hundred and under one thousand words, two dollars; of over one thousand words, three dollars.

For copies of drawings, the reasonable cost of making them.

SEC. 4935. Patent fees may be paid to the Commissioner of Patents, or to the Treasurer or any of the assistant treasurers of the United States, or to any of the designated depositories, national banks, or receivers of public money, designated by the Secretary of the Treasury for that purpose; and such officer shall give the depositor a receipt or certificate of deposit therefor. All money received at the Patent Office, for any purpose, or from any source whatever, shall be paid into the Treasury as received, without any deduction whatever.

SEC. 4936. The Treasurer of the United States is authorized to pay back any sum or sums of money to any person who has through mistake paid the same into the Treasury, or to any receiver or depository, to the credit of the Treasury, as for fees accruing at the Patent Office, upon a certificate thereof being made to the Treasurer by the Commissioner of Patents.

TRADE-MARK.

TITLE LX, Rev. Stat., Chap. 2, p. 963:

SEC. 4937. Any person or firm domiciled in the United States and any corporation created by the authority of the United States, or of any State or Territory thereof, and any person, firm, or corporation resident of or located in any foreign country which by treaty or convention affords similar privileges to citizens of the United States, and who are entitled to the exclusive use of any lawful trade-mark, or who intend to adopt and use any trade-mark for exclusive use within the United States, may obtain protection for such lawful trade-mark by complying with the following requirements:

First. By causing to be recorded in the Patent Office a statement specifying the names of the parties, and their residences and place of business, who desire the protection of the trade-mark; the class of merchandise and the particular description of goods comprised in such class, by which the trade-mark has been or is intended to be appropriated; a description of the trade-mark itself, with facsimiles thereof, showing the mode in which it has been or is intended to be applied and used, and the length of time, if any, during which the trade-mark has been in use.

Second.—By making payment of a fee of twenty-five dollars in the same manner and for the same purpose as the fee required for patents.

Third.—By complying with such regulations as may be prescribed by the Commissioner of Patents.

SEC. 4938. The certificate prescribed by the preceding section must, in order to create any right whatever in favor of the party filing it, be accompanied by a written declaration verified by the person, or by some member of the firm or officer of the corporation by whom it is filed, to the effect that the party claiming protection for the trade-mark has a right to the use of the same, and that no other person, firm, or corporation has the right to such use, either in the identical form or in any such near resemblance thereto as might be calculated to deceive; and that the description and facsimiles presented for record are true copies of the trade-mark sought to be protected.

SEC. 4939. The Commissioner of Patents shall not receive and record any proposed trade-mark which is not and cannot become a lawful trade-mark, or which is merely the name of a person, firm, or corporation unaccompanied by a mark sufficient to distinguish it from the same name when used by other persons, or which is identical with a trade-mark appropriate to the same class of merchandise and belonging to a different owner, and already registered or received for registration, or which so nearly resembles such last-mentioned trade-mark as to be likely to deceive the public. But this section shall not prevent the registry of any lawful trade-mark rightfully in use on the eight day of July, eighteen hundred and seventy.

Sec. 4910. The time of the receipt of any trade-mark at the Patent Office for registration shall be noted and recorded. Copies of the trade-mark and f the date of the receipt thereof, and of the statement filed therewith, under the seal of the Patent Office, certified by the Commissioner, shall be evidence in any suit in which such trade-mark shall be brought in controversy.

Sec. 4911. A trade-mark registered as above prescribed shall remain in force for thirty years from the date of such registration; except in cases where such trade-mark is claimed for and applied to articles not manufactured in this country and in which it receives protection under the laws of any foreign country for a shorter period, in which case it shall cease to have any force in this country by virtue of this act at the same time that it becomes of no effect elsewhere. Such trade-mark during the period that it remains in force shall entitle the person. firm, or corporation registering the same to the exclusive use thereof so far as regards the description of goods to which it is appropriated in the statement filed under oath as aforesaid, and no other person shall lawfully use the same trade-mark, or substantially the same, or so nearly resembling it as to be calculated to deceive, upon substantially the same description of goods. And at any time during the six months prior to the expiration of the term of thirty years, application may be made for a renewal of such registration, under regulations to be prescribed by the Commissioner of Patents. The fee for such renewal shall be the same as for the original registration; and a certificate of such renewal shall be issued in the same manner as for the original registration; and such trade-mark shall remain in force for a further term of thirty years.

Sec. 4912. Any person who shall reproduce, counterfeit, copy, or imitate any recorded trade-mark and affix the same to goods of substantially the same descriptive properties and qualities as those referred to in the registration, shall be liable to an action on the case for damages for such wrongful use of such trade-mark, at the the suit of the owner thereof; and the party aggrieved shall also have his remedy according to the course of equity to enjoin the wrongful use of his trade-mark and to recover compensation therefor in any court having jurisdiction over the person guilty of such wrongful use.

Sec. 4913. No action shall be maintained under the provisions of this chapter by any person claiming the exclusive right to any trade-mark which is used or claimed in any unlawful business, or upon any article which is injurious in itself, or upon any trade-mark which has been fraudulently obtained, or which has been formed and used with the design of deceiving the public in the purchase or use of any article of merchandise.

SEC. 4944. Any person who shall procure the registry of any trade-mark, or of himself as the owner of a trade-mark, or an entry respecting a trade-mark in the Patent Office, by making any false or fraudulent representations or declarations, verbally or in writing, or by any fraudulent means, shall be liable to pay any damages sustained in consequence of any such registry or entry, to the person injured thereby; to be recovered in an action on the case.

SEC. 4945. Nothing in this chapter shall prevent, lessen, impeach, or avoid any remedy at law or in equity, which any party aggrieved by any wrongful use of any trade-mark might have had if the provisions of this chapter had not been enacted.

SEC. 4946. Nothing in this chapter shall be construed by any court as abridging or in any matter affecting unfavorably the claim of any person to any trade-mark after the expiration of the term for which such trade-mark was registered.

SEC. 4947. The Commissioner of Patents is authorized to make rules, regulations, and prescribe forms for the transfer of the right to the use of trade-marks, conforming as nearly as practicable to the requirements of law respecting the transfer and transmission of copyrights.

CHAP. 301.—AN ACT TO AMEND THE LAW RELATING TO PATENTS, TRADE-MARKS, AND COPYRIGHTS.

Be it enacted by the Senate and House of Representatives of the United States of America in Congress assembled. That no person shall maintain an action for the infringement of his copyright unless he shall give notice thereof by inserting in the several copies of every edition published, on the title page or the page immediately following, if it be a book; or if a map, chart, or musical composition, print, cut, engraving, photograph, painting, drawing, chromo, statue, statuary, or model or design intended to be perfected and completed as a work of the fine arts, by inscribing upon some visible portion thereof, or of the substance on which the same shall be mounted, the following words, viz.: "Entered according to act of Congress, in the year ——, by A. B., in the office of the Librarian of Congress, at Washington;" or, at his option, the word "Copyright," together with the year the copyright was entered, and the name of the party by whom it was taken out; thus—" Copyright, 18—, by A. B."

SEC. 2. That for recording and certifying any instrument of writing for the assignment of a copyright, the Librarian of Congress shall receive from the persons to whom the service is rendered, one dollar; and for every copy of an assignment, one dollar; said fee to cover, in either case, a certificate of the record, under seal of the Librarian of Congress; and all fees so received shall be paid into the Treasury of the United States.

SEC. 3. That in the construction of this act, the words "engraving," "cut," and "print" shall be applied only to pictorial illustrations or works connected with the fine arts, and no prints or labels designed to be used for any other articles of manufacture shall be entered under the copyright law, but may be registered in the Patent Office. And the Commissioner of Patents is hereby charged with the supervision and control of the entry or registry of such prints or labels, in conformity with the regulations provided by law as to copyright of prints, except that there shall be paid for recording the title of any print or label not a trade-mark, six dollars, which shall cover the expense of furnishing a copy of the record under the seal of the Commissioner of Patents, to the party entering the same.

SEC. 4. That all laws and parts of laws inconsistent with the foregoing provisions be and the same are hereby repealed.

SEC. 5. That this act shall take effect on and after the first day of August, eighteen hundred and seventy-four.

Approved, June 18, 1874.

REPEAL PROVISIONS.

TITLE LXXIV, Rev. Stat., p; 1091:

SEC. 5595. The foregoing seventy-three titles embrace the statutes of the United States general and permanent in their nature, in force on the 1st day of December, one thousand eight hundred and seventy-three, as revised and consolidated by the commissioners appointed under an act of Congress, and the same shall be designated and cited, as the Revised Statutes of the United States.

SEC. 5596. All acts of Congress passed prior to said first day of December, one thousand eight hundred and seventy-three, any portion of which is embraced in any section of said revision, are hereby repealed, and the section applicable thereto shall be in force in lieu thereof; all parts of such acts not contained in such revision, having been repealed or superseded by subsequent acts, or not being general or permanent in their nature: *Provided*, That the incorporation into said revision of any general and permanent provision, taken from an act making appropriations, or from an act containing other provisions of a private, local, or temporary character, shall not repeal, or in any way affect any appropriation, or any provision of a private, local or temporary character, contained in any of said acts, but the same shall remain in force; and all acts of Congress passed prior to said last named day no part of which are embraced in said revision, shall not be affected or changed by its enactment.

SEC. 5597. The repeal of the several acts embraced in said revision shall not affect any act done or any right accruing or accrued, or any suit or proceeding had or commenced in any civil cause before the said repeal, but all rights and liabilities under said acts shall continue, and may be enforced in the same manner as if said repeal had not been made; nor shall said repeal in any manner affect the right to any office, or change the term or tenure thereof.

SEC. 5598. All offenses committed, and all penalties or forfeitures incurred under any statute embraced in said revision prior to said repeal, may be prosecuted and punished in the same manner and with the same effect as if said repeal had not been made.

SEC. 5599. All acts of limitation, whether applicable to civil causes and proceedings, or to the prosecution of offenses, or for the recovery of penalties or forfeitures, embraced in said revision and covered by said repeal, shall ·not be affected thereby, but all suits, proceedings or prosecutions, whether civil or criminal, for causes arising or acts done or committed prior to said repeal, may be commenced and prosecuted within the same time as if said repeal had had not been made.

SEC. 5600. The arrangement and classification of the several sections of the revision have been made for the purpose of a more convenient and orderly arrangement of the same, and therefore no inference or presumption of a legislative construction is to be drawn by reason of the title under which any particular section is placed.

SEC. 5601. The enactment of the said revision is not to affect or repeal any act of Congress passed since the 1st day of December, one thousand eight hundred and seventy-three, and all acts passed since that date are to have full effect as if passed after the enactment of this revision, and so far as such acts vary from, or conflict with, any provision contained in said revision, they are to have effect as subsequent statutes, and as repealing any portion of the revision inconsistent therewith.

Approved, June 22, 1874.

AN ACT TO PUNISH THE COUNTERFEITING OF TRADE-MARK GOODS AND THE SALE OR DEALING IN OF COUNTERFEIT TRADE-MARK GOODS.

Be it enacted by the Senate and House of Representatives of the United Ssates of America in Congress assembled, That every person who shall with intent to defraud, deal in or sell, or keep or offer for sale, or cause or procure the sale of, any goods of substantially the same descriptive properties as those referred to in the registration of any trade-mark, pursuant to the statutes of the United States, to which, or to the package in which the same are put up, is fraudulently affixed, said trade-mark, or any colorable imitation thereof, calculated to deceive the public, knowing the same to be counterfeit or not the genuine goods referred to in said registration, shall, on conviction thereof, be punished by fine not exceeding one thousand dollars, or imprisonment not more than two years, or both such fine and imprisonment.

SEC. 2. That every person who fraudulently affixes, or causes or procures to be fraudulently affixed, any trade-mark registered pursuant to the statutes of the United States, or any colorable imitation thereof, calculated to deceive the public, to any goods, of substantially the same descriptive properties as those referred to in said registration, or to the package in which they are put up, knowing the same to be counterfeit, or not the genuine goods, referred to in said registration, shall, on conviction thereof, be punished as prescribed in the first section of this act.

SEC. 3. That every person who fraudulently fills, or causes or procures to be fraudulently filled, any package to which is affixed any trade-mark registered pursuant to the statutes of the United States, or any colorable imitation thereof, calculated to deceive the public, with any goods of substantially the same descriptive properties as those referred to in said registration, knowing the same to be counterfeit, or not the genuine gooods referred to in said registration, shall, on conviction thereof, be punished as prescribed in the first section of this act.

SEC. 4. That any person or persons who shall, with intent to defraud any person or persons, knowingly and willfully cast, engrave, or manufacture, or have in his, her, or their possession, or buy, sell, or offer for sale, or deal in, any die or dies, plate or plates, brand or brands, engraving or engravings, on wood, stone, metal, or other substance, moulds, or any false representation, likeness, copy, or colorable imitation of any die, plate, brand, engraving, or mould of any private label, brand, stamp, wrapper, engraving on paper or other substance, or trade-mark, registered pursuant to the statutes of the United States, shall upon conviction thereof, be punished as prescribed in the first section of this act.

SEC. 5. That any person or persons who shall, with intent to defraud any person or persons, knowingly and willfully make, forge, or counterfeit, or have in his, her, or their possession, or buy, sell, offer for sale, or deal in, any representation, likeness, similitude, copy, or colorable imitation of any private label, brand, stamp, wrapper, engraving, mould, or trade-mark, registered pursuant to the statutes of the United States, shall, upon conviction thereof, be punished as prescribed in the first section of this act.

SEC. 6. That any person who shall, with intent to injure or defraud the owner of any trade-mark, or any other person lawfully entitled to use or protect the same, buy, sell, offer for sale, deal in or have in his possession any used or empty box, envelope, wrapper, case, bottle, or other package, to which is affixed, so that the same may be obliterated without substantial injury to such box or other thing aforesaid, any trade-mark, registered pursuant to the statutes of the United States, not so defaced, erased, obliterated, and destroyed as to prevent its fraudulent use, shall, on conviction thereof, be punished as prescribed in the first section of this act.

SEC. 7. That if the owner of any trade-mark, registered pursuant to the statutes of the United States or his agent, make oath, in writing, that he has reason to believe, and does believe. that any counterfeit dies, plates, brands, engravings on wood, stone, metal, or other substance, or moulds of his said registered trade-mark, are in the possession of any person, with intent to use the same for the purpose of deception and fraud, or makes such oaths that any counterfeits or colorable imitations of his said trade-mark, label, brand, stamp, wrapper, engraving on paper or other substance, or other substance, or empty box, envelope, wrapper, case, bottle. or other package, to which is affixed said registered trade-mark not so defaced, erased, obliterated and destroyed as to prevent its fraudulent use, are in the possession of any person, with intent to use the same for the purpose of deception and fraud, then the several judges of the circuit and district courts of the United States and the Commissioners of the circuit courts may, within their respective jurisdictions, proceed under the law relating to search-warrants, and may issue a search-warrant authorizing and directing the Marshal of the United States for the proper district to search for and seize all said counterfeit dies, plates, brands, engravings on wood, stone, metal, or other substance, moulds, and said counterfeit trade-marks, colorable imitations thereof, labels, brands, stamps, wrappers, engravings on paper, or other substance, and said empty boxes, envelopes, wrappers, cases, bottles, or other packages that can be found ; and upon satisfactory proof being made that said counterfeit dies, plates, brands, engravings on wood, stone. metal, or other substance, moulds, counterfeit trade-marks, colorable imitations thereof, labels, brands, stamps, wrappers, engravings on paper or other substance, empty boxes, envelopes, wrappers, cases, bottles or other packages, are to be used by the holder or owner for the purposes of deception and fraud, that any of said judges shall have full power to order all said counterfeit dies, plates, brands, engravings on wood, stone, metal, or other substance, moulds, counterfeit trade-marks, colorable imitations thereof, labels, brands, stamps, wrappers, engravings on paper or other substance, empty boxes, envelopes, wrappers, cases, bottles, or other packages, to be publicly destroyed.

SEC. 8. That any person who shall, with intent to defraud any person or persons, knowingly and willfully aid or abet in the violation of any of the provisions of this act, shall, upon conviction thereof, be punished by a fine not exceeding five hundred dollars, or imprisonment not more than one year, or both such fine and imprisonment.

Approved August 14, 1876.

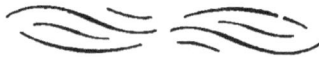

www.ingramcontent.com/pod-product-compliance
Lightning Source LLC
Chambersburg PA
CBHW021637270326
41931CB00008B/1055